Along The Way
Blue Ridge Scenic

Trip Guide

Rick Straub with Ron Wallace

Copyright ©2007 Rick Straub
ISBN-13 : 978-0-9793269-0-5
ISBN-10 : 0-9793269-01

Published by Rick Straub
Printed in the United States
Distributed by Blue Ridge Scenic Railway

Trip Date _____

Conductor _____

Contents

Acknowledgements 3
Introduction 4
History 6
Signs 10
Mileposts 11
Along The Way
    Blue Ridge Station 15
    Murphy Junction 19
    Mineral Bluff 21
    Kodak Moment 23
    Curtis Switch 25
    Galloway 27
    Fish Trap 29
    Toccoa Bridge 31
    McCaysville/Copperhill 33
    Hook & Eye 35
Consist
    2007 consist...................................... 37
    Snow Train... 39
    Locomotives 41
    Coach 105/106 43
    Coach 2705.. 45
    Coach 549 47
    Concession 206 49
    Concession 114 51
    Coach 332.. 53
    Coach 150.. 55
    Open-Air 2975/2929 57
    Open-Air 697 59
Vintage Railroad
    Horn Signals 62
    Ticket Punch / Pocket Watch 63
    Conductor's Cap/Communications/Crew .. 64
    Squeal of the wheels 65
    Gauge... 66
    Hobo Signs.. 67
    Ticket to Ride 68
    Railroad Safety... 69
    Logo 70
    Volunteers 71
    Group Photo.. 73
    Air Brakes.. 75
    Terms 76

Acknowledgements

Over the last 25 years there have been so many people involved in bringing back the rail to the North Georgia Mountains, literally hundreds! From Politicians and local citizens to retirees and rail fans, most of them volunteers, people near and far played a very important part. Thanks for all your time; it was worth the effort.

Thanks to all those folks who helped in the preparation of this book by reviewing, correcting, providing feedback, and support. I appreciate your time.

A special thanks to Ray Leader who not only contributed material to the project, he was instrumental in getting it published.

Thanks to Wilds L. Pierce whose enthusiasm and sponsorship made production possible.

As anyone who has ridden the engine knows Engineer Carl Hyman provides plenty of good conversation. During one of my trips in 2006 he introduced me to the idea of a trip guide that started this project.

My wife Rae Ann was excited about the idea from day one and was always supportive as I continually pestered her with ideas, revision after revision.

I hope Y'all enjoy what I have put together.

- Conductor Rick

Introduction

Welcome to *Along the Way Blue Ridge Scenic Trip Guide,* We are glad you have chosen to ride with us today. Every day is a great day for a train ride!

Trip guides are not unique at all; they started when the railroads began to stretch out into remote areas and needed to provide visitor services, and increase their revenue. Works such as *Harpers New-York and Erie Rail Road Guide,* of 1855-6 or *Crofutt's Trans-continental Tourist Guide,* of 1872 provided a view from the rails over the countryside, man-made bridges, viaducts, and landscape that had never been imagined before. Full of advertisements that helped cover the cost of production, they were usually sponsored by the railroad. Many years later guides open a window into what life was like back then. Long distance or day trips, these places were illustrated by wonderful art work, replaced today by digital camera's that someday will serve as a snapshot of our time.

Along the Way Blue Ridge Scenic is structured like a self-guided tour. It will give you information about railroads, the Blue Ridge Scenic Railway (BRSR) line between Blue Ridge, GA. and McCaysville, GA. / Copperhill, TN. and assist you with identifying points of interest. It picks up where the old line leaves off in the current day 2007 with a revitalized tourist line over historic track in the North Georgia Mountains and gives you some tools to make your trip informative and fun.

In current tourist excursions across the country many of us are volunteers who love being part of recovering the past while helping you enjoy the present. Since BRSR had its first trip the train crew has been made up of volunteers. This guide contains information gathered from many sources and used over the years by the volunteers for the enjoyment of visitors, passengers, and rail fans. The 2007 operating season will mark the tenth year of service and this guide is one way to celebrate the accomplishments of so many. We have made every effort to supply correct and valuable information to the reader. If you find anything incorrect and can verify facts, we would be happy to consider revising.

Many of you will be experiencing a train for the first time; others will conjure up memories while making new ones. Whichever it is, sit back, relax for a moment, enjoy yourself, and the ones you're with.

Our journey today will take us from Blue Ridge, GA. (1680 ft. above sea level) and follow the Toccoa River north descending 220 feet into McCaysville, GA. / Copperhill, TN. (1460 ft. above sea level). This thirteen and a half mile trip takes about one hour by rail. Depending on the time of year and amount of foliage you will get a different view on every trip. Riding in an open-air or coach car will also provide a different ride. All of the cars are different and unique.

Let's get started!

History

The city of Blue Ridge in its prime during the late 1800's and early 1900's depended on the railroad (like many other communities) to bring tourists and travelers. Passenger service ended with the last run on February 28, 1949. The four-lane highway passed by the outskirts and many people never ventured downtown. The train station was no longer the center of attention, as it once was. More than thirty years passed before this sleepy mountain town would start its transformation.

Starting around 1980 a group of citizens in Blue Ridge started work to restore the Blue Ridge Station in an effort to bring folks downtown and preserve the historic landmark. Around this time CSX Transportation Inc. (CSX) sold the 8 miles of rail between Ellijay and Blue Ridge to the state of Georgia. In 1987 CSX sells the 41 miles of track between Marietta and Tate and leased 31 miles between Tate and Ellijay to a group of investors to form Georgia Northeastern Railroad (GNRR). In 1990 the original investors sell all interests in GNRR to the current owners.

In 1988 the Great Smoky Mountain Railroad (GSMR), in Bryson City and Dillsboro North Carolina began a successful passenger operation which suggested that running a tourist train could help save a portion of the old Atlanta to Knoxville Railroad. This section of track running between Blue Ridge and McCaysville follows the Toccoa River through some historic and scenic countryside. CSX wanted to abandon the line from Blue Ridge to McCaysville because of taxes and maintenance requirements. The Blue Ridge Depot and Park were acquired by the city. A group of citizens from Fannin County approached

Wilds L. Pierce, the majority stockholder of Georgia Northeastern Railroad Company, Inc. (GNRR) about support to help save this portion of track and start a scenic railroad.

The management of GNRR contacted the Atlanta Chapter, National Railroad Historical Society (NRHS) to solicit their help in providing experienced excursion personnel to help staff the trains. Larry Dyer and Ray Leader of the Atlanta Chapter, NRHS were able to determine that the venture had a high possibility of success and have the chapter involved again in passenger excursions. The response was to form a committee and develop a tourist railroad. Invited were two members of the Atlanta Chapter NRHS, two members from the community, and two from GNRR.

The committee worked through the details necessary to create a viable organization. An early decision was made to incorporate this entity as the Blue Ridge Scenic Railway (BRSR), a subsidiary of the GNRR. Dick Hillman, Safety Director for the GNRR was named as the first General Manager of BRSR and arranged to have the logo created which is still in use. Keith Douglas was the GNRR VP for Operations and would be in charge of all operational areas.

In the 1996, the right-of-way was acquired by the State of Georgia. On May 3, 1997, a group of railroad enthusiasts, members of the Atlanta Chapter NRHS, and local members of the North American Railcar Operators Association (NARCOA) joined GNRR to start clearing the line beyond Ellijay. Six miles of fallen limbs, kudzu overgrowth, and trees growing between the ties were cleared by hand as the first step. Then GNRR began track repair.

June 1988 was set for the first trip and just two weeks prior to opening day a many decades old wooden trestle just north of Ellijay was "struck by lightning" and burned down leaving only two rails hanging in space. This meant all of the equipment in Tate, GA. and Elizabeth, GA. had to be shipped on CSX Line via Cartersville, GA. to Etowah, TN. and then over to McCaysville, GA. In addition, more vandals released handbrakes on a train at Keithsburg, GA. that caused a derailment and destruction of two locomotives and seven grain cars. Meanwhile, other efforts were continuing in preparation for a startup date.

GNRR was busy working on track repairs, purchasing and leasing passenger cars and constructing boarding areas at Blue Ridge Station and in McCaysville behind the Masonic Lodge. The Atlanta Chapter, NRHS was busy recruiting and drafting the first safety manual, training volunteers to staff the trains as Car Hosts, Conductors and Trainmen. Carl Hymen was hired by GNRR as the first Engineer for the BRSR. Del and Diane Kittendorf were recruited to assist with training while Diane served as the first Volunteer Coordinator. Ray Leader was qualified as first Conductor and served as Chief Conductor for many years. The Atlanta Chapter's Commissary (Concession) car #206 was leased and added to the train consist. Car #206 was staffed by chapter members, with all profits going back to the Southeastern Railway Museum in Duluth, GA.

On Saturday, May 30, 1998 the first tourist excursion was made between Blue Ridge and McCaysville as a VIP trip with a second trip on Sunday, May 31st. June 6, 1998 was opening day for operations. Initially most of the Car Hosts and Concession Crew were

Atlanta Chapter members. That has shifted over the years to be mostly local volunteers. The first season consisted of 79 trips carrying 17,000 passengers.

Over the next several years the schedule has been modified with some specials runs, school trips and regular Santa Trains that always sell out. In 1998 the train consisted of three coach cars, one open air, and one concession. In 2006 the train consisted of six coach cars, three open air-cars, and one concession.

Since that time thousands of visitors have made the trip and many found the area a great place to call home. Railroad excursions have exploded with popularity across the country as more folks look for events the entire family can enjoy; both young and old. By 2004 general building projects were underway in McCaysville / Copperhill and Blue Ridge. Now restaurants, antique shops and other businesses are once again thriving in both cities. The surrounding mountains have remained a popular vacation retreat. Cabins and property development has brought more people during the holidays and prompted special runs and extended seasons.

In the beginning the railroad brought life to the area and like so many places around the country, it once again breaths life into the community. The efforts of those so many years ago have paid off by preserving this piece of rail history for everyone to share. Had that track been pulled up like the Murphy branch, it would have been lost forever but instead it continues to serve. 2007 marks the 10th operating season. It's an exciting time for the railroad.

Signs

There are many signs along the way. The horn, whistle and flashing lights are a warning system that is vital to maintaining safety. The Engineer controls are on the right side of a forward moving locomotive. The Trainmen sits on the left watching for anything out of the normal. The public must co-exist with trains and it is important that everyone does their part to ensure safety. Watch for these signs along the route.

Crossings

Marked by the "W" Whistle Post, "X" indicates more than one. The Horn is blown four (4) times starting 1000 feet from the crossing until covered while ringing the engine bell.

Speed

Reduce Speed Signs are yellow and numbered. Speed restrictions are set by the maintenance crew.

End Restriction Signs are green. Resume speed after rear the of the train has passed the green marker.

Safety, Safety, Safety –

At the beginning of each day and when changing control from one locomotive to another, the Brake Test sign is a caution. This indicates the train could move and everyone should stand back. At no time should anyone except the Trainmen board the train when this sign is displayed. The test only takes about 15 minutes.

Mileposts

Mileposts are markers placed at one-mile intervals beginning at company headquarters and extending to the end of the line, hence the name. Since our line was part of the Louisville & Nashville Railroad (L&N), our mileposts begin at Louisville, Kentucky. As we depart Blue Ridge (~395.5) on our journey to McCaysville/Copperhill, the mile markers are on the west (or left) side of the train. They are white posts with a number on them.

The first milepost or marker we come to will be 395 and is located a short distance across from Mountain Street at what used to be a wood yard. From 1999 until 2005 there were about 5 log cars a week pulled south to connect with CSX. One log car can hold 5 truck loads of logs.

Markers 393/384 are really old wooden markers. They are the only two left over from the "OLD" days. Marker 385 has almost been destroyed and is now marked with a metal sign. The concrete marker is there, but in bad shape.

Use the milepost to determine points along the way. Each point of interest on the next few pages will give you a number and approximate time from departure at Blue Ridge to help you find them.
Use these symbols to help determine where you are by time and mile marker.

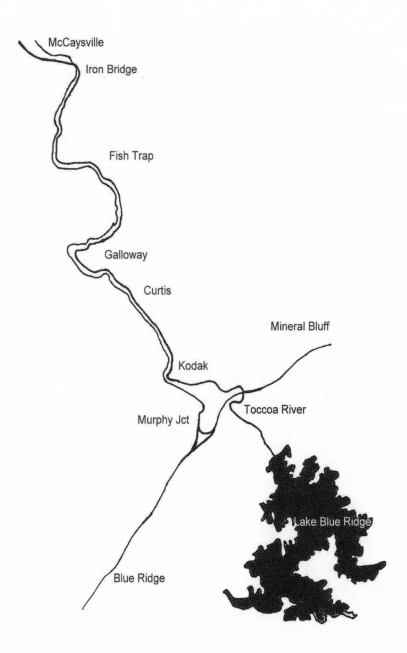

Mile Posts

Along The Way

The Ten (10) minute warning is indicated by four (4) long blasts of the train horn . — — — —

This is also the call to return from the McCaysville/ Copperhill layover.

The Floor Plan of Blue Ridge Station describes the structure almost identical to the "Standard Plan Special Combination Station" that L&N built in the early 1900's. A frame struc-

ture built in 1906 with a slate roof, weather board exterior, office and waiting rooms ceiled.

The Blue Ridge Station served cross purpose with the city as a restaurant and community center for many years. Starting around 1980, fund-raising began to refurbish this depot. The Green Thumb Project donated time, money, and labor along with senior citizens and citizens of Blue Ridge. Sandpaper and steel wool were used on the walls of the freight room and broken windows were replaced with glass from the Store House Building (now Hallmark). The Chamber of Commerce visited the depot museum in Etowah where they

were given the original exterior color scheme. This is also where the 1905 build date came from that appears on the plaque out front.

Cleaning and repairs allowed the Blue Ridge Station to be the first structure in the

city of Blue Ridge to be placed on historical registry (1982 - Building - #82002413). A Quilt hangs in the gift shop with all the names of those people and businesses who participated in the project to restore the Blue Ridge Train Station.

The committee was afraid that CSX Transportation would pull up the track (and dash any possibility of re-use) and they wanted the location to always look like a real train station complete with track and cars. It took the largest crane anyone had ever seen to lift the caboose from the main line to the section of rail it now sits on. Georgia DOT finally bought the track between Blue Ridge and McCaysville and leased it back to GNRR for the Blue Ridge Scenic Railway.

After the restaurant moved out in 1998 the building was once again selling train tickets. Today the entire building is used for the train tourist business but that was not always the case. It started small and grew into a facility serving thousands of guests each year coming through this small community. The freight room is now the depot gift shop. The caboose is used by the crew and the box car is the Hometown Project office.

Flag Stop
In rural areas passengers wanting to board the train had to flag the train down in order for it to stop.

Depot
A building for the accommodation and protection of railway passengers and freight .

Station
A stopping place where trains regularly come to stand for the convenience of passengers, take on fuel, and move freight.

Train Station
A facility where passengers may board or disembark from the train and goods may be loaded or unloaded. It usually consists of one building for passengers and goods plus others associated with functioning of the railway.

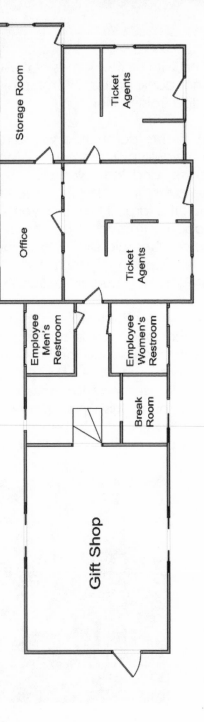

17   Trip Guide

"Conductor to GNR 7529,
We're all buttoned up back here,
Hand brake released
Ready to proceed north to McCaysville."

"Here we go!" ——

Along The Way

Just across from the Industrial Park crossing there is a set of tracks that veer off to the right. This is Murphy Junction. The tracks run along the Hogback Ridge and go to Mineral Bluff, Georgia and at one time continued on to Murphy, North Carolina. The Murphy Branch supplied the only means of delivering food, clothing and rebuilding materials to Asheville, North Carolina and surrounding communities after the 1916 hurricane. The tracks have been removed between Mineral Bluff and Murphy.

A "WYE" is a track arrangement with three switches and three legs for reversing the direction of a train. The intersection of Murphy Junction is where three sets of tracks come together. This unique configuration allows moving a piece of On Track Equipment (OTE) through and back out facing in a different direction. Flipping the OTE is important if a cargo door must align with a loading platform or a locomotive needs to be facing another direction.

A spur or sidetrack is a short stretch of railway used to store or enable trains on the same line to pass. There are several side tracks between Blue Ridge and Murphy Junction that are used for storage and building the train consist. There is only one WYE on this line.

Mineral Bluff

When the railroad arrived in 1886 the area known as Blue Ridge was just a grassy field, beautiful and natural. Mineral Bluff got the areas first train station a year after the track reached that point. A brick structure built in 1887 was influenced by locals to support a large tannery and timber products. Visitors would come for the healthy mineral springs and inspirational spa retreats. The track ends just beyond the depot, removed between here and Murphy, NC. What was once a main line is now a branch line used occasionally for storing rolling stock. The depot has been refurbished but you will have to drive to Mineral Bluff a short distance up the highway to see how the renovations are progressing.

11/11/2006

Hogback Ridge Road followed the rail to
Mineral Bluff but now the bridge is no longer passable.
One side sits on private property out of reach of visitors.

Twenty minutes out we come to what is referred to as "The Kodak Moment". This point in our travel is located at mile marker 392, which is only a short distance beyond what used to be a "Petting Farm." This is the point in which we first encounter the Toccoa River. It is called the "Kodak Moment" because it is quite picturesque and you can see both up and down the river as it is in a sharp curve to the right.

The river at this point is known as the Toccoa River and this section starts at the dam of Lake Blue Ridge, flowing in a northerly direction until it crosses the Georgia / Tennessee State line. When the water passes under the iron bridge in McCaysville, which denotes the state line, the river becomes the Ocoee River. The Ocoee River, as you remember, was the venue for the Kayaking and Canoeing events of the 1996 Atlanta Summer Olympics. After passing through the Ocoee River Gorge, the water joins the Hiawassee River. The Hiawassee River joins the Tennessee River, flows west to Chattanooga then down into Alabama. The Tennessee River flows across Alabama to Mississippi where it turns northward again, flowing across the entire state of Tennessee to where it joins the Ohio River at Paducah, Kentucky. The Ohio River flows west to join the Mississippi River at Cairo, Illinois where it turns south to complete its travel through Memphis, Baton Rouge, New Orleans, and to the Gulf of Mexico.

Along The Way

Curtis Switch

Curtis Switch Road is a gated crossing. Once a meeting place for north and south bound trains it had a side track where one train could wait for the other. Just past the road on the right is an old foot bridge for crossing the river.

Flashing red lights, lowered crossing gates, and a ringing bell at a road crossing are classic warnings associated with railroads. There are three gated crossings where you can wave to the waiting cars.

Head on Collision

On July 8, 1928, around 8:51 PM there was a head-end collision between two L&N passenger trains about a mile south of Curtis. North bound Train #6 pulled by Engine 139 collided with south bound Train #7 pulled by Engine 137 which resulted in the death of an engineer. At the time it was a single-track line operated by timetables and train orders.

A single track between Blue Ridge and McCaysville means that coordination must be made to insure two pieces of equipment do not occupy it at the same time. An Absolute Block is a block (area between two mile markings) that may be occupied by only one train at a time. Absolute Block authority is granted to BRSR for movements in both directions. This means that no other equipment will share the track with us today.

Watch for mile post 390 on the way back to Blue Ridge. There will be a perfect photo opportunity just past Curtis Switch Road. The track sweeps to the right and then back to the left for a view of the entire train.

11/11/2006

Along The Way

Galloway

A short distance from Curtis Switch Road (about 1½ miles) at what would be mile marker ~388.5 the river curves to the right. This low area is reported as having the first white settlers in the area. Not only did the river supply fish for food in addition to what they could grow but also transportation.

In 2003 the railroad arranged for volunteers to have a picnic on this site by the river.

Blue Ridge Scenic Railway

Blue Ridge Scenic Railway
241 Depot Street
Blue Ridge, Georgia 30513

Phone: 1-800-934-1898
Local: 706-632-9833
E-mail: brscenic@tds.net
www.brscenic.com

40

Between mile post 386 and 387, we come to the "Fish Trap". This is one of the most interesting and fascinating sights on our trip. It is constructed of river rock from both sides of the river about a third of the way across the river, and then a deep "V" is formed pointing downstream. It is not known exactly by who or when "Fish Traps" were constructed. They were in the rivers when the first settlers came to the area. It is generally accepted that early Indians would enter the river upstream, then walk, splash or in other ways cause a commotion in the water, causing the fish to swim down stream to get away from the commotion. The fish would be concentrated in the "V" area where they could be caught in nets and baskets. Fish Traps are not unique to our river. They were common in most of the rivers across the Southeast.

Occasionally when the water is high, usually controlled by Blue Ridge Dam, it's a little harder to see.

DEPOT GIFT SHOP

Conveniently located in the Blue Ridge Station cargo room accessible from the deck.

There are some items stocked on the concession car but for a better selection of items come by and see us before or after your trip.

Authorized "Walthers" dealer for model railroad supplies

Blue Ridge Scenic Railway
241 Depot Street
Blue Ridge, Georgia 30513

Toccoa Bridge

50

At mile marker 384, we cross the Toccoa River on our way to McCaysville/Copperhill. Markers 384 along with 393 are wooden markers as discussed earlier. The railroad, then known as the M&NG (Marietta and North Georgia) reached McCay in the summer of 1889. The route of the railroad was to be from Marietta, Georgia to Knoxville, Tennessee. With crews working both north from Marietta and south from Knoxville, the two sections of track were joined on June 30, 1890 amid much celebration. On July 4, 1890 a passenger train traveled the entire line from Marietta to Knoxville for the first time. Regularly scheduled service began on August 18, 1890. The M&NG became the AK&N (Atlanta, Knoxville and Northern) Railroad in the late 1890's and then in 1902 the line was purchased by the L&N (Louisville and Nashville). In 1905, the L&N began a program of upgrading the newly acquired railroad, which included replacing the bridge across the Toccoa River south of Copperhill. This bridge is of heavier construction than other bridges along the line.

The bridge spanning the Toccoa River offers a beautiful view both up and down the river as you cross. During the summer months you can wave to rafters and tubers enjoying the water ride.

Along The Way

Just as the river changes its name at the state line, so does the name of this small mountain community. McCaysville/Copperhill grew up around the railroad and mines a few miles away. The mines produced copper, iron, sulfur, zinc and small amounts of gold and silver. Before 1900 the Copper Basin was the largest mining district in the Southeast. The mines have long since gone (closed in 1989) but the town is still serving visitors and tourists. In 1990 the area suffered a great flood when the banks of the river overflowed several feet up building walls.

A favorite for travelers is to take a picture while standing in two states at the same time using the painted line in the IGA parking lot. Today there are shops and restaurants to visit while in town. Be sure to get a walking map to assist your tour.

Upon anticipation of the train a loading area was constructed behind the Masonic Lodge. Steps on the north side provided access to the side walk. The Blue Ridge Scenic Railway McCaysville pavilion (75 Toccoa Ave.) was opened in the summer of 2005. The old house that occupied this space was replaced by a facility much more suited to the visitor providing rest rooms and tables. It has a wooden ramp to the sidewalk.

Hook and Eye

The famous Hook and Eye Division of the Louisville & Nashville Railroad (L&N) was the first to tackle the Appalachian Barrier in the South. It gets its name from two engineering feats. At a time in the South after the Civil War when money was in short supply, curves were cheaper than cuts.

The "Hook" is a 15-degree double reverse-curve at Tate Mountain in Georgia that took four miles to gain two and a half miles "as the crow flies" between Talking Rock and Whitestone.

The "Eye" is a spiral loop that crosses under itself 7/8 mile long coming very close to crossing itself twice as it traverses Bald Mountain in Tennessee. A 1940 Railroad Magazine article Hook and Eye Division by H.G. Monroe, states "Where else can a hogger watch the rear of his train with as little effort as on the Hook and Eye?" It was built around 1898 replacing six miles of reckless rail constructing the great W switchback that allowed the rail to drop seventy five feet to the bank of the Hiawassee River. Before the loop only 4 cars at a time could be shuttled between each leg.

Very few features of this type existed on a U.S railroad at the time but the Eye still exist today. In 2007 with the cooperation of the Tennessee Valley Railroad Museum working with their Hiawassee River Rail Adventures ("HRRA"), The Blue Ridge Scenic Railway cars will be part of two scheduled trips to Gee Creek, Tennessee over this historic and famous Eye portion of the old L&N "Hook and Eye Division" track.

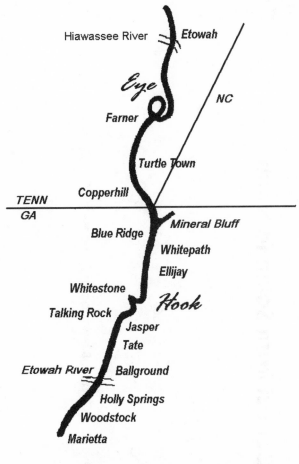

The "Hook & Eye" Division

This image was redrawn based on a drawing that appeared in the 1940 magazine article by H.G Monroe

2007 Consist from South to North

On-Track-Equipment	8704 or 2000	*106	*105	2705	*549	114 or 206	*332	150	2975	*2929	697	7529
Seating	2	50	50	60	56	~	50	65	70	70	45	3
Type	L	C	C	C	C	B	C	C	O	O	O	L

L = Locomotive, C = Coach, B = Baggage Concession, O = Open-Air

* Restrooms

The Consist

(pronounced CON-sist) the cars which make up a train.

Every vintage car is different and unique with its own history. While on board the train feel free to visit the Concession (Commissary) car where you will find drinks, snacks, and souvenirs. If you haven't already, be sure to visit the Depot Gift Shop in the Blue Ridge Train Station.

Snow Train

It was a winter morning in the mountains like many others. My wife Rae Ann and daughter Carley were hoping for snow. About 8AM Sunday morning we woke to flurries that quickly subsided, just another teaser. The plan was for them to go back to Atlanta while I worked the train and followed later. They left about 9AM, the snow started to fall again about 9:30AM and it didn't stop for what seemed like hours.

Several inches fell quickly and continued once the base had formed. Making my way to Blue Ridge would be slow and cautious. Erma Gladieux was the office manager and took this wonderful picture of the south end of the train that appeared in the 2001 brochure and calendar. Many of the reservations were cancelled, but the scheduled trip departed Blue Ridge station on time. All of the businesses were closed including the ticket office so everyone could go for a snow ride.

Notice the tracks are showing through the snow and what has collected on the nose of the locomotive appears to be slipping. By departure time the temperature was high enough to start the snow melting even though flurries continued. By the time the train got back to Blue Ridge Station that afternoon 80% of the snow had melted into streams of water running down the roads. Since that day we have not seen a repeat of the amount of snow on a single day in the mountains, however, we are still hopeful. - *Rick Straub*

Photo by Erma Gladieux

A new breed of workhorse, the "chopped-nose" GEEP was introduced in the 1950's by General Motors - Electro Motive Division (GM-EMD).

In the Georgia Northeastern Railroad (GNRR) fleet, we at the BRSR have used locomotives GNR-7529 at the north end of the consist pulling us to McCaysville, and GNRR-7562 at the south end pulling us back to Blue Ridge. Some day it would be nice to do some switching at each location but for now there is no place to turn around so we will pull up, change locomotive control and pull back, that's why they have a locomotive at each end. Both units came from Conrail.

Between 1954 & 1959 GM-EMD produced a number of model GP9 , 1750 HP locomotives. In 1976 Conrail inherited a fleet of GP9 locomotives from Penn Central that were rebuilt as GP10's. GNR-7529 started out as New York Central NYC-5958, later renumbered to PC-7358 by Penn Central, CR-7358 by Conrail, and then CR-7529 as a GP10. GNR-7562 started out as Pennsylvania Railroad PRR-7098, later renumbered to CR-7098 by Conrail, and then CR-7562 as a GP10.

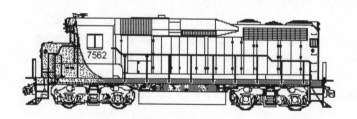

Front Cover photo by Rick Straub. 2002 GNRR locomotive 7562 sitting idle at rock quarry in White Path. Back cover photo from GNRR calendar by Martin O'Toole.

The Consist

Coach 105/106

Coach 106 was one of 42 10-roomette 6 bedroom sleepers "ten-six sleepers" built by Pullman Standard and delivered to the Florida East Coast (FEC) Railroad September of 1949. They carried the name "Oriente" until it was purchased by the Canadian National (CN) Railroad in 1967 when FEC cut passenger service. Renamed "Grande Riviere" and eventually converted to present long-distance coach configuration, with the number CN/VIA 5740 still evident on the inside doors at the end of the car. Later CN sold it to Bangor & Aroostook Railroad where it was renamed BAR 106.

In 2001 it was acquired by Blue Ridge Scenic Railway to be used as first-class service. Originally powered by 114 volt DC provided by batteries and a genemotor driven by a 480v three phase AC motor. The genemotor was driven by the rotation of the cars axles through gears while the car was underway.

BRSR converted to onboard diesel powered generator in 2001 by employees of GNRR, contractors, and volunteers. It was extensively rewired and air-conditioning completely replaced. These 80ft. cars seat 50 passengers . 105 is the sister to 106.

Photo by Larry Heron

The Consist

Coach 2705

Coach 2705 was purchased from the Long Island Railroad (LIRR) when it was retired in 1999. It has its own generator for heat and air-conditioning.

It was built by Pullman-Standard in 1963 as a 130 seat MU (cab control) commuter coach. In 1973, it was converted to an 86 seat coach, commuter bar (push-pull)

Some cleaning was performed and modification made to fit our needs. Originally a 3/2 seating configuration with five seats across. Many of the seats were removed to allow more leg room than was needed for a commuter as well as increasing the center aisle width by using only two seats on each side. The excess seats that came from modifications to cars 2705/2929/2975 were used in Coach 332 to make it more comfortable.

Photo by Larry Herron

The Consist

Coach 549

Coach 549 was purchased by Blue Ridge Scenic Railway in 1998 from Greensboro, North Carolina Chapter of the National Railway Historical Society (NRHS). This passenger car was built 1938 by Budd Mfg. for the Atchison, Topeka and Santa Fe Railroad. It operated in various passenger train assignments including the famous Santa Fe Super Chief, operating between Chicago and Los Angeles, until being sold to Penn Central Railroad. Last regular service was with New Jersey Transit in commuter service into New York City until being retired and sold to the Greensboro, North Carolina chapter of the NRHS.

Since the car has been in the BRSR consist several modifications have been made. Two additional restrooms are located at the north end and a storage room at the south end now houses the air system. Ceiling fans were added before the air-conditioning was replaced.

Photo by Larry Herron

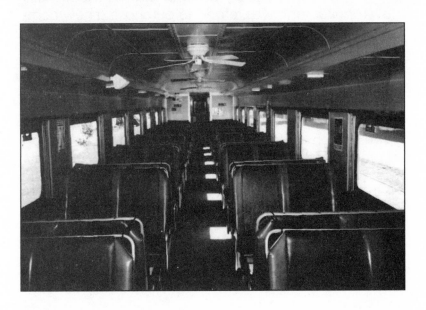

The Consist

Concession 206

Concession 206 was built for the Northern Pacific Railroad as part of an order of 10 baggage cars numbered 200 thru 209. It was ordered in November 1955 and delivered in May 1956 by Pullman-Standard. It was originally built as a 70 ft. baggage car but in 1958 had a small bathroom (messenger) installed in the center of the car. Northern Pacific retired the car from active service in 1971 but held and used it occasionally as a commissary (concession) car in excursion service for approximately 10 years then sold it to a passenger car dealer in Portland, OR.

In the mid-1980s, following a derailment of the NS steam excursion fleet, the company imposed a requirement of roller bearings and tight-lock couplers on all excursion equipment. The Atlanta Chapter, NRHS which had a commissary car that did not meet these new requirements was forced to purchase a new commissary car which was 206. When purchased, the car was painted in Burlington Northern green and had no generator, AC or counters in it. The car was used in NS steam excursion and New Georgia RR trips until both programs ended in late 1994. The car was leased to the Blue Ridge Scenic Railway in 1998 and used for three seasons. The Atlanta Chapter has had the car on its property since then as a gift shop and now it's back. Car 206 was purchased by Blue Ridge Scenic Railway as the second concession car in 2006.

Ever since acquiring commissary car #206 in 2006 folks have been having some fun with what has been stenciled on the undercarriage "**DO NOT HUMP**".

There are two different types of railroad classification yards, flat and hump yards. In a hump yard, a hill is made so that the engines can push the cars up and across, and when they reach the top, they're uncoupled and allowed to drift down the correct track by gravity to the train that they will go out on. A worker in a nearby tower use buttons or levers to throw switches and direct to the proper train.

The problem with hump yards is the coupling is often quite rough and fragile items can be broken. It was typical to have "DO NOT HUMP" stenciled on office cars, dining cars and any other car with fragile items so they would not be sent down to a rough couple. The reason they're used is that it's faster than having an engine gently connect each car.

Concession 114

The Brittany, Concession #114 on the consist was manufactured by National Steel Car Co in May, 1958 for the Canadian National Railway Co. as car CN/VIA 9293. In 1974 it was renumbered to CN/VIA 9664. When it was eventually bought by the Bangor & Aroostook Railway Co in Maine it became BAR 114.

It was purchased by Blue Ridge Scenic Railway in 2000 to act as its concession car. In April 2001, it was revamped with counters and coolers to its current configuration by volunteers. The concession is essential to the train consist. It contains the communications center, souvenirs, drinks and snacks (popcorn and candy). Connected to land power by night it also carries its own generator. It has gated sliding doors on each side but no steps. Connected between 332 on the north and 549 on the south end we use the hand brake while standing in McCaysville.

The Consist

Coach 332

Coach CSTX 972332 (commonly referred to as 332) was purchased by Blue Ridge Scenic Railway after being retired from service by CSX Transportation. Built by American Car Foundry in 1955 as a 60 seat divided (probably Jim Crow) coach for the L&N RR. It was acquired by Amtrak in 1971 then retired in 1976 and sold to CSX for work train service and numbered 972332. May have been one of the last "Jim Crow" cars built. Finally it was restored to coach service in 1998, one of original cars in the consist.

Before renovations by BRSR it had no seats so we installed bus seats for a couple of years. Since then a few changes have been made by the volunteers. The seats were replaced by excess ones pulled from the Long Island Commuter cars and the table was split in two with each half attached to a side. Restrooms were added to the north end and shelves with baby changing area added to original restroom space. Coach 332 is used for the crew briefing before each scheduled trip, it is connected to the north end of the commissary and its generator supplies electricity to the remaining north consist.

Toccoa River

Photo by Larry Herron

The Consist

Coach 150

Coach #150 (Lake Blue Ridge) was originally built for New York Central Railroad, in 1923 by Osgood Bradley Company which was later taken over by Pullman. This car was purchased by Blue Ridge Scenic Railway in 1998 from Gettysburg Railroad.

The car has "walk-over" seats so the direction of the car could be changed at the end of the line but have been tied down so they don't get worn-out. The upholstery has been refinished and the windows are now locked down to avoid injury and allow the heat and air (that was recently added) to work properly. The 80 ft. car was originally built as a self-propelled electric commuter car with controls in the Vestibule. It had open windows in the summer and electric baseboard heat in the winter, got power from a thin rail beside the regular rail. On the north end you can identify where a window has been covered with a metal plate on the left side and a jump seat folds out of the wall on the right side.

Railroad coaches with pairs of seats on each side of center aisle, and open interior are know as 'American Style' coach. Coach 150 seats 65 passengers and the closest restroom is on 332 to the south.

Lake Blue Ridge

Photo by Larry Herron

Open-Air 2975/2929

Open-Air cars 2929 and 2975 were among three Pullman-built push-pull coaches (2929, 2975, and 2705) purchased from the Long Island Rail Road (LIRR) when they were retired in 1999. "In 1954, the LIRR ordered twenty-five 120-seat commuter cars from Pullman-Standard. An additional fifty-five identical cars were ordered in June 1955. The first order, car numbers 2901-2925, were delivered from Pullman-Standard's Osgood Bradley plant in Worcester, Mass. in June, 1955 as lot 6961, drawing W-52607".

Two LIRR cars 2929 (Ridge Runner) and 2975 (River Breeze) were converted to open-air by volunteers Scottie Wershing, Joe Beardon, Carl Hymen and Chuck Nutting. Torches were used to remove the car's 24 double windows and to cut larger openings in order to widen the view. They used torches but didn't know what to expect so they had fire extinguishers and water buckets ready. Extra support posts were welded in place as well as safety rails along the sides to fully transform it to an open-air car. Existing seats were removed and replaced with steel-framed padded benches that run lengthwise through the middle of the car. Coach 2705 remains its original design although some of the seats were removed for more comfort. Look for the New York State seal pattern imprinted in the ceiling.

Photo by Larry Herron

The Consist

Open-Air 697

Our first open-air car was purchased from The Great Smoky Mountain Railroad in 1998. We lovingly refer to it as 697. The Alarka Creek is a 40 ft. box car built in 1971 converted to open-air coach with retractable stairs on each side with seating down the middle facing out the sides. As with all cars it has its own unique ride, sitting closest to the north engine it relays the sounds of the bell, horn and rails better than any other car. Car 697 was originally isolated from the rest of the train. Car Hosts had to keep a cooler to sell drinks, and passengers had to wait until the end of each trip to use any facilities.

The steps were lowered and raised by a hand crank until they were removed prior to the 2005 season. In 2004 a walkway was fashioned to connect the car to the rest of the consist and passengers are no longer restricted. Car 697 gets the most action as well. When the consist is built (sometimes weekly) it couples to the north locomotive to pull the train off the house track. When trainman training is performed car 697 is used for practice coupling. The first cars to fill up are always the open-air cars so 697 is regularly filled to capacity.

Photo by Larry Herron

The Consist

Vintage Railroad

Horn Signals

SOUND	SIGNAL (HORN) INDICATION
0 = short blast — = long blast	Meaning
0	Applying air brakes
— —	Proceeding releasing air brakes
0 0	Acknowledging any signal not otherwise provided for
0 0 0	Backing up
0 — —	Acknowledging train order signal displayed for delivery of orders
0 0 0 0	Calling for signals (10 minutes warning)
— — 0 —	Approaching public crossings at grade, tunnels, yards, or other points where men may be at work and when passing the rear of freight trains
0 —	Inspect train for a leak in brake pipe system or for brakes sticking
Succession of short sounds	Warning to people and/or animals

Ticket Punch

Ticket punching began in the 1860's in the United States. The conductor or someone on his behalf would cancel out the passenger ticket by punching a hole into it. The conductors hole punch was a vital form of identification, each conductor had his own specifically shaped hole punch to identify them. It was  up to the conductor to ensure that every passenger paid proper passage as this revenue was important.

Ticket punching is still used today but on the tourist excursions it is mostly for fun and educational purposes, however it sometimes brings a smile especially when we do NOT throw people from the train.

Pocket Watch

Most recognizable by the chain hanging from the conducts vest pocket is the pocket watch. It is very important the conductor and engineer keep the same time throughout the run; the crew  regularly synchronize their time pieces to a standard clock. Every crew member is expected to supply their time piece and is responsible for its accuracy. The railroad in 1883 brought standardized 'Railroad time' and the four time zones we use in the United States. Before the standard, cities kept local time and coordination for long distances was almost impossible. There were several train crashes involving trains keeping different times.

Conductor's Cap

The Conductor can be recognized by the "badge of office" traditional black hat with gold trim. A symbol of the passenger train conductor and used throughout North America starting in the 1870's. Other trades such as porter or agent as well as trolley car operators use the same style cap.

Communications

Radios are regularly used in connection with train operations. On a train that consists of ten 80ft. cars the engineer cannot see everything that is happening on the ground at the opposite end or inside the cars so his instructions must be clear and expected. The crew meets before each trip to discuss assignments and plans for the day; the Conductor coordinates all these activities. Hand signals as they were used long ago are still an option should radio communications be interrupted. The crew must first meet and agree on a plan that hand signals will then be used. Part of the regular rules training each year is going over the hand signals in case they're needed.

Crew

The crew today will consist of an Engineer, who is an Employee of Georgia Northeastern Railroad and operates the locomotive. There are several Safety Car Hosts who assist with loading, promote safety, and answer questions. The Conductor is in charge of the train, responsible for the safety of its passengers, crew, and public relations. There are also two or more Trainmen recognizable by wearing black hats who assist with train operations and movement, One trainman rides in the engine while the other calls signals to the engineer in route from inside the train. Operating crews have to take annual classroom instruction and pass a safety operating rules test.

Squeal of the wheels

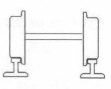

You may notice a squealing sound, as if the engineer is riding the brakes. This squealing sound is notice- able as the train rounds a curve, and as you well know, there are many of those on our trip. The fact is.... This is not the brakes at all; instead, it is the flanged wheels of the car rubbing against the inside crown of the rail. Why does this happen? Under each car is a set of "trucks" upon which the car rides. Our cars have two axle trucks, which means that there are two axles af- fixed together to form a single unit. The length of the truck assemblies, combined with the length of our cars and the sharpness of the curves, means that as the train rounds a curve opposite corners of the flanged wheels of the truck rub against the inside crown of the rail, causing the squealing sound. One might rightfully wonder that if there is that much squealing, there must be quite a bit of wear and friction involved. This is true. If there is wear and friction, then the obvious solution is to oil or grease the rubbing surfaces. This also is true. Yes... the track crew does indeed grease the rails in areas that rubbing and friction occur.

Gauge

The gauge is the distance between the inside edges of the rail. The U.S. as well as three-fifths of the world uses Standard Gauge (4 ft. 8.5 in. or 1.4 meters). This odd number was brought to us from Britain in 1829 when locomotives were imported and the rails had to match.

Vehicles such as chariots, carts or carriages in early transportation were pulled primarily by horses. The speed at which the vehicles could travel, weight a horse could pull, and arrangement that could be handled by a single driver dictated the width of the axle. Later tramways were built with the same gigs and tools that were used to build wagons. So the locomotives built by the British were made with these same measurements. Later American technology enhancements continued to use this common length.

Narrow gauge used in the U.S. in the last decade of the 19th century measured 3 ft 6 in. and in many cases only 2ft. The benefits are shorter-radius turns, cheaper to build and operate. On the down side narrow gauge can only handle lower hauling capacity at slower speeds.

The original line used today was built as narrow gauge and then upgraded much later to standard gauge. Since money was scarce as it was for many railroads across the country at that time, our route took many turns to avoid obstacles because it was cheaper to go around rather than through them. This was one of the key reasons for the original line to be abandoned yet makes it perfect for tourism. Our passenger cars are longer today and have speed restrictions that make it perfect for taking a leisure trip that gives plenty of time for pictures.

Hobo Signs

A Hobo was an independent and resourceful person who travels for work. The American Hobo "Knights of the road" communicated through a system of marks (Hobo Signs). This code gave information or warnings to others. Written in chalk or coal they let fellow Hobos know what to expect. We have produced only one here for fun at the holding tank dump location depicting bad water.

During the early 1880's times were hard and no one had the money to go places or pay for a ticket to get there. Hobo's took to the rails in great numbers and people in rural communities would help by giving them jobs during harvest time. During the great depression they depicted a way of life many Americans could relate to as thousands of women and children also traveled the rails.

They lived in camps, did not use real names (although some became famous) and followed rules. There was no breaking into homes or threatening people. Offenses could bring heavy punishment by fellow hobo's . Extensive information is available on the internet for those interested.

Mulligan stew (hobo stew) was made from the combined contributions of any Hobo who wanted to eat some. A pot of stew was refreshed by a scrap of meat, a biscuit, or wilted vegetables from a garden. The Hoboes essentials were most importantly water and something to start a fire with but also included a can opener, a knife, a spoon, and candles.

"King of the Road" was a song by Roger Miller that depicted a lifestyle but the name was also an honor given by unofficial vote of the Hoboes on the road that is the best educated, experienced and most respected of all.

Ticket to Ride

There is no assigned seating in any of the cars. We do however suggest changing sides on the way back so that everyone gets an opportunity to see all of the sights. So come aboard, settle in and meet some new friends.

```
BRSR welcomes        800-934-1898        XV
STRAUB/PASSES
              FRIDAY, 11:00am
                  VOLUNTEER

May 07, 2004 OPEN AIR 2975
Boarding 10:40 am              69938-1    69938-1

                                          05/07/04
1-800-934-1898    VISIT DEPOT GIFT SHOP
```

Tickets are only good for the date printed and you must ride in the car assigned because so many trips sell out. The car number and boarding time also appear on the ticket. Keep it handy as the conductor will come around once we leave the station to punch it out. Be sure to hang on to your stub, it will be a great addition to your scrap book.

Throughout the years many of the local businesses in the area have supported the railroad by giving discounts on meals or merchandise to ticket holders. Ask your car host what businesses are participating in discounts at the time of your ride, show them the stub and save some money.

Reservations are not required but it is highly recommended to pre-purchase and pick-up before the trip, that way you are assured of a Ticket to ride.

Railroad Safety

The Cross Buck sign is a warning to the public of a rail crossing. Some crossings have gates, lights and bells to warn the public of an oncoming train. Often we forget that train tracks are private property, here long before other vehicles, and trains always have the right of way. When crossing tracks at designated locations we need to be conscious of safety.

Trains can move at anytime; never crawl under or between cars. This is one of the most dangerous things anyone can ever do and we see more adults do it every year. It is so important to slow down and think about your actions. The result could ruin a perfectly good day for everyone. So we must reach out to the children to help teach their parents what they have learned about railroad safety in school, it is dangerous and stupid to go under the train.

Putting coins on the rail is another bad idea. Rather than smashing a piece of metal it can become a projectile.

We at BRSR are proud of our perfect safety record and we need your help to keep it. Equipment can always be replaced, people cannot.

Logo

In 1998 when the BRSR logo was first created the printer said the train that appears in the center would not be very defined so it was removed. The logo was not the same without the train on it so it was added back in 2000. The logo without the train appeared again in the 2003 brochure.

As we prepare for the 2007 season the logo will be enhanced with "10th Season Anniversary" on the bottom and the years "1998-2007" at the top. This leaves three version of the railway logo.

Before the season has started, Ron Huster has already made changes to his jacket.

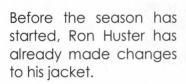

Volunteers

Everyone except the engineer and concession staff are volunteers. Ever since the idea immerged to start up a tourist excursion volunteers have played a vital part. They shared a love for railroading and a common goal to help re-establish a line in the North Georgia Mountains. In the early years, it was mostly Atlanta Chapter NRHS members but has shifted to more local residents in current years. There are many of the original group that still comes back year after year. We also see new faces every year.

They have helped maintain, rework, and clean some of the equipment and enjoyed special trips, deck parties and luncheons over the years. But every-one keeps coming back because it is fun, relaxing and we are family. If you would like to become part of the family, you will be welcomed. Just make it known you are interested to any of the crew and we will put you in touch with the Volunteer Coordinator.

Each volunteer starts off with some basic train-ing, and what to expect on a trip as a Safety Car Host. The Car Host assists passengers on and off the train while visiting and providing information during the jour-ney. Each trip starts with a safety briefing to reinforce our training. After you have gotten the routine down and are interested in some additional responsibilities you are welcome to attend a yearly training session and become qualified as trainmen. It's not for every-one and many of the volunteer's just love the freedom and less time commitment of being a Car Host. Either way we want people to enjoy working all the positions of the crew. After you have become an accomplished Trainman you can choose to qualify as Conductor. That's all it takes, a little time and commitment. For your time and commitment you also receive benefits so don't hesitate to ask a volunteer for more information.

I became a volunteer in the year 2000 when my friend Del Kittendorf convinced me it was fun and worthwhile stating in his words "there is not a better bunch of folks to work with." My family and I volunteered together coming into the mountains enjoying the scenery, local activities, and camaraderie. I took the additional training and worked my way from Trainman to Conductor over the next few years. Where else can someone with a computer background get to work with vintage locomotives? The folks at GNRR have worked with us year after year to give us the foundation needed to safely run the train. We trade off jobs with experienced Conductors so that everyone gets an opportunity to learn and gain their own experience.

One memorable trip for me was a log run south out of Blue Ridge to Tate with five loaded log cars. Calvin Lee, Carl Hyman and I encountered several empty gravel cars along the way that we had to shove several miles before the train could be reconfigured at the rock quarry. After switching cars around by GNRR we were on our way pulling five loaded log cars and three full gravel cars up the hill past Twin Mountain Lake in Talking Rock almost to Tate. The load was too much for two locomotives on this particular day and a third locomotive was brought down to assist. We never made it to Tate that hot summer day. Calvin lost his fight with cancer several years later but I will always remember him and that trip as a highlight of my railroad adventures.
–Rick Straub

Group Photo

The group photo has been a tradition over the past few years. Taken at the first rules training course of the season, led by our behind-the-scenes coach and engineer Jeff Knowles. This is your 2007 qualified Trainmen and Conductors.

Reading from left to right.

First Row:
Jonathan Deitch , Anne Hymen , Rae Breed
Pat Brady , Lora Huster , Larry Dyer

Second Row:
Ron Huster , Bruce Fielding , Ron Wallace
Don Anderson , Leonard Zeh , Jack Warner
David Ashworth, Del Kittendorf

Third Row:
 Ray Leader, Joe Brandon, Chuck Nutting , Pat Moore
Judy King , Ron Graner, Dick Wood, Dick Burnett
John Davis , Bob Brackett , Rick Straub

Back Row:
Bob Ciminel, Mike Morrey, Jeff Knowles, Don King
Barry Vincent

Not Pictured:
Ron Long, Charles Garland, Scottie Wershing
Bill Purdy , David Shuman

Air Brakes

The first train brakes required a brakeman. To stop a train the engineer would blow a certain pattern with the whistle and the brakemen would move from car to car setting handbrakes. The first air brakes used a compressor and a pipe running the length of the train. In this direct brake system, when the brake pipe was pressurized the brakes went on.

The modern air brakes have an inverted behavior of the direct brake. By pressurizing the brake pipe or charging the system causes the brakes to release. A triple valve is attached to the brake pipe, then to a reservoir, and to the brake cylinder. As air is pumped by the locomotive, the triple valve directs it into the car's reservoir. When fully charged the reservoirs will be at a pressure of 70 pounds. We test the brakes before every trip ensuring the ability to apply and release on every car.

To apply the brakes the air is removed from the brake pipe. When the reservoir air pressure is greater than the brake pipe pressure it moves the triple valve and allows pressure into the brake cylinder, and the brakes apply.

To release the brakes an increase in pressure greater than the 70 pounds in the reservoir causes the triple valve to a position that allows air in the brake cylinder to escape and the brakes are released. In essence, the brakes are always applied; it takes effort to release them. By placing the train into emergency the air in the brake pipe is instantly released causing rapid application of the brakes.

In addition to the air each car is equipped with a hand brake that is set when we tie the train down for the night. Once the engineer blows the whistle telling us its safe to disembark, the passengers exit the train and the crew shuts everything down.

Terms

Railroad workers as well as hobos had their own language. Here are a few terms just for fun but if you are interested in learning more about railroads there are many sites on the internet that cater to enthusiasts.

A-No.1 -"number one man" , later came to mean, "all right (or okay) with me." , thumbs up
Adam and Eve on a raft - Two fried eggs on toast. "Wreck 'em" if they are scrambled. "With their eyes open," if not
Alligator bait - Fried or stewed liver. Too costly for hobos
Axle grease - Butter. Sometimes called plaster.
Brakemen – Baby Lifter
Caboose – Brain box
Coffin nail -- cigarettes.
Conductor – ram-rod, skipper, the brains, No sweat
Deadhead – RR employee traveling as a passenger.
Engineer – Hogger, Hoghead
Foamer -- from FOMITE " Fanatically Obnoxious Mentally Incompetent Train Enthusiast"
Gandy dancer - Railroad worker who laid sections of rail
Grade -- The ratio of elevation gained or lost per distance traveled measured in feet, expressed as a percent "%".
Hog – Locomotive
Knuckle – movable portion of the drawbar coupler
Old Head – One who has been around long enough to become familiar with his work or who 'has his head cut in' knows how to do his job well.
Piglet – Engineer Trainee

Georgia Northeastern Railroad

Georgia Northeastern Railroad
109 Marr Av. NW
Marietta, GA 30060
770-428-4784
http://www.gnrr.com/

The Georgia Northeastern Railroad, Inc. (GNRR) operates ~100 miles of trackage from our interchange with CSX Transportation at Marietta, to McCaysville, Georgia. We occupy the old Louisville and Nashville Railroad's "Hook And Eye" line.

We are classified by the Association of American Railroads as a "shortline railroad" This classification is based on annual revenues and car loadings. As a shortline railroad, we are in a position to be highly flexible in terms of our ability to customize our service to each and every customer. Within this mileage, we presently provide service to 29 customers that ship or receive a wide variety of products, and each of which requires unique rail service.

We operate the Blue Ridge Scenic Railway presenting riders with a journey along the Toccoa River in the beautiful North Georgia Mountains. The GNRR is locally owned. Its 25 employees are all local folks, and you will find that doing business with us is a real pleasure.

We are always anxious to have potential customers check with our present customers to learn first hand how customized personal service can enhance their business. The GNRR has rail accessible industrial sites available along our trackage and we would be glad to show sites to you for potential rail use.

Thanks for riding with us today.

I hope this guide added to a pleasurable trip. Until we see you again, have a safe journey and remember, it's always a great day for a train ride.

About The Authors

Rick Straub joined the volunteer team in 2000, A Conductor since 2001. He started the volunteer newsletter in 2005 and has helped introduce technology to improve operations. Now living in the North Georgia mountains with his wife Rae Ann and daughter, Carley.

Ron Wallace joined the volunteer team in 2001. A contributing author to the volunteer newsletter and Conductor, he has served as Host Coordinator and General Manager over the last few years.